Come Aside and Rest Awhile

A book of family prayer

edited by
JOSEPH G. KELLY

illustrated by
COLLEEN KELLY SPELLECY

EMMAUS
BOOKS

PAULIST PRESS

IMPRIMATUR
✠ Joseph L. Hogan
Bishop of Rochester

November 20, 1976

Copyright © 1977 by
Joseph G. Kelly

All rights reserved. No part of this book may be reproduced or transmitted in any form or by any means, electronic or mechanical, including photocopying, recording or by any information storage and retrieval system, without permission in writing from the Publisher.

Library of Congress
Catalog Card Number: 76-24441

ISBN: 0-8091-1988-9

Cover Photo: Regina Siwek Shreter

Published by Paulist Press
Editorial Office: 1865 Broadway, N.Y., N.Y. 10023
Business Office: 545 Island Road, Ramsey, N.J. 07446

Printed and bound in the
United States of America

ACKNOWLEDGMENTS

We wish to express our gratitude to the following for permission to quote from the indicated works:

The Grail, from *The Psalms. A Singing Version* by Paulist Press, by special arrangement with Wm. Collins & Sons. Ltd.

Greek Orthodox Archdiocese of North and South America, from *Orthodox Prayer Book*, 1944.

Hebrew Publishing Co., from *Blessings and Hymns for Various Occasions*, by D. Josephson, 1932.

Morehouse-Barlow Co., Inc., from *Prayers for Every Occasion*, edited by Frank Colquhoun.

International Commission on English in the Liturgy, Inc., from English translation of excerpts from the Roman Missal and from Evening Prayer and Night Prayer of the Liturgy of the Hours. Copyright © 1973, 1975, International Committee on English in the Liturgy, Inc. All rights reserved.

Geoffrey Chapman Publishers, from *A Book of Evening Prayers*, two hymns by Reverend James Quinn.

Jerome Leaman, for his prayer, as published in the Liturgy of the Hours.

Contents

Introduction 1

Evening Prayer to Our Father 5

Evening Prayer to the Holy Trinity 13

Compline 21

Vespers 29

Thoughts for Evening Meditation 39

Litanies of Praise 55

Evening Prayer for the Sabbath 71

Prayers for Special Evenings 77

Other Prayers for Evening 85

For
M. Genevieve
who first taught us to pray

Introduction

Prayer is both the joy and duty of every Christian. Because of this, prayer books have always been a part of the Christian tradition.

Since Vatican Council II, much attention has been given to liturgical prayer. Time has been spent reworking the Lectionary and the Sacramentary used at the Eucharist. The Office books used by priests and religious for their common prayer have also been revised. But for the great majority of faithful Christians, evening prayer comes at the very end of a hectic day when, for a few brief moments spent alone or with one's family, God is praised and thanked in a very simple manner. This little book is for those people.

The need for brevity and simplicity, however, should not mean being deprived of the richness of the Judeo-Christian religious heritage. Thus I have made a special effort to make use of the Psalms of the Old Testament, the Canticles of the New Testament, and the evening hymns used in the early Church. I have also attempted to preserve some of the beauty of the ancient formats, making use of Jewish, Roman Catholic and Orthodox traditions.

I have included in the book four set arrangements for evening prayer. Although they are not lengthy, each one is meant to be complete in itself. But this is not done to restrict you. Feel free to mark certain favorites or those most conducive to your own prayer and then arrange your own combination. The additional single prayers at the end of the volume may also be used in any combination. You will also find included a special section of thoughts to help your evening meditation as well as several ancient litanies which the Church has long used to sing the praises of the Father, Jesus and the Mother of God. Finally, you will find special prayers for the Sabbath and for Christmas and Easter evenings.

A special thank you to the Sisters who were students in my classes at Our Lady of Mercy Motherhouse during the summer of 1975. They spent several weeks using the beginnings of this little book and made excellent suggestions for its improvement. I am also grateful to my wife, Pat, whose loving support and skills helped to make this project possible.

All of this is presented as a help to prayer, never forgetting that it is the Spirit who prays through us. Blessed be God.

St. Bernard's Seminary
Rochester, New York
2 May 1976

Evening Prayer to Our Father

This prayer, adapted from the Jewish tradition, praises God, the King of the universe.

(In beginning, pause for a few moments and recall that you are in the presence of God.)

Blessed are you, O Lord our God, King of the universe, who makes the bands of sleep to fall upon my eyes and slumber upon my eyelids. May it be your will, O Lord my God and God of my fathers, to allow me to lie down in peace and to let me rise up again in peace. Let not my thoughts trouble me, nor fearful dreams, but let my rest be perfect before you. Enlighten my eyes, lest I sleep the sleep of death, for it is you who gives light to the apple of the eye. Blessed are you, O Lord, who gives light to the whole world in your glory.

PSALM 4

When I call, answer me, O God of justice;
from anguish you release me, have mercy and hear me.

O men, how long will your hearts be closed,
will you love what is futile and seek what is false?

It is the Lord who grants favors to those whom he loves;
the Lord hears me whenever I call him.

Fear him, do not sin: ponder on your bed and be still.
Make justice your sacrifice and trust in the Lord.

'What can bring us happiness?' many say.
Lift up the light of your face on us, O Lord.

You have put into my heart a greater joy
than they have from abundance of corn and new wine.

I will lie down in peace and sleep comes at once,
for you alone, Lord, make me dwell in safety.

Cause us, O Lord our God, to lie down in peace and raise us up, O our King, to life. Spread over us the tabernacle of your peace. Direct us aright through your own good counsel. Save us for your name's sake and be a shield about us. Remove from us every enemy and war, every sickness, hunger and sorrow. Shelter us beneath the shadow of your wings, for you, O God, are our guardian and our deliverer; yes, you, O God, are a gracious and merciful King. Guard our going out and our coming in, and give us life and peace from this time forth and forevermore.

PSALM 121

I lift up my eyes to the mountains:
from where shall come my help?
My help shall come from the Lord
who made heaven and earth.

May he never allow you to stumble.
Let him sleep not, your guard.
No, he sleeps not nor slumbers,
Israel's guard.

The Lord is your guard and your shade;
at your right side he stands.
By day the sun shall not smite you
nor the moon in the night.

> it is through man the cantor of the universe, that the secret cosmic prayer is disclosed.
>
> — A. HESCHEL

The Lord will guard you from evil,
he will guard your soul.
The Lord will guard your going and coming
both now and forever.

Blessed be the Lord by day; blessed be the Lord by night; blessed be the Lord when we lie down; blessed be the Lord when we rise up. For in your hands are the souls of every living thing, and the spirit of all human flesh. Into your hands I commend my spirit; you have redeemed me, O Lord, God of truth. Our God in heaven, assert the unity of your name, establish your kingdom continually, and reign over us forever and ever.

PSALM 16:5-11

O Lord, it is you who are my portion and cup;
it is you yourself who are my prize.
The lot marked out for me is my delight:
welcome indeed the heritage that falls to me.

I will bless the Lord who gives me counsel,
who even at night directs my heart.
I keep the Lord ever in my sight: since
he is at my right hand, I shall stand firm.

And so my heart rejoices, my soul is glad;
even my body shall rest in safety. For
you will not leave my soul among the dead,
nor let your beloved know decay.

You will show me the path of life,
the fullness of joy in your presence,
at your right hand happiness forever.

CLOSING VERSES

For your salvation, I hope, O Lord.
   I hope, O Lord, for your salvation.
   O Lord, for your salvation, I hope.

No, he sleeps not nor slumbers, Israel's guard.

The Lord bless you and keep you:
   The Lord make his face to shine upon you
   and be gracious to you;
   the Lord turn his face to you
   and give you peace.

Fear him, do not sin:
   ponder on your bed and be still.

Evening Prayer to the Holy Trinity

Christians of the Orthodox tradition give us this model of prayer which praises the Triune God.

OPENING VERSES

Every evening will I bless you,
  and I will praise your name forever and ever.

For with you is the fountain of life,
  and in your light we see light.

Blessed are you, O Lord, the God of our fathers.
  Praised and glorified is your name forever. Amen.

PRAYER TO THE HOLY SPIRIT

Heavenly King and Comforter, Spirit of Truth present everywhere, who fills all creation, the treasure of all blessings and giver of life, come and dwell within us. Purify us and save our souls, O gracious God.

IN PRAISE OF THE TRINITY

Holy God, Holy and Mighty, Holy and Immortal,
  have mercy on us.

Lord, cleanse our sin.
Master, forgive our transgressions.
Holy One, visit us and heal our infirmities,
  for your name's sake.

Glory be to the Father
  and to the Son
  and to the Holy Spirit,
  now and ever
  and for all ages. Amen.

A HYMN OF PRAISE

Glory to God in the highest,
  and peace to his people on earth.

the spirit helps us
in our weakness
for
we
do
not
know
how
to
pray
as
we
ought.

ROMANS 8:26

Lord God, heavenly King,
almighty God and Father,
   we worship you, we give you thanks,
   we praise you for your glory.
Lord Jesus Christ, only Son of the Father,
Lord God, Lamb of God,
you take away the sin of the world:
   have mercy on us;
you are seated at the right hand of the Father:
   receive our prayer.
For you alone are the Holy One,
you alone are the Lord,
you alone are the Most High,
   Jesus Christ,
   with the Holy Spirit,
   in the glory of God the Father. Amen.

EVENING PRAYER

At this hour which marks the end of the day, O God my Lord, I come before you again in thankfulness to glorify your name. You have watched over me through the day and now your protection, O Lord, I seek throughout the night. Send me calm rest to restore my body and soul, and strengthen my faith in you. When I arise in the morning, render me worthy to pray again to you and glorify your holy name of the Father and of the Son and of the Holy Spirit. Amen.

PETITIONS TO THE TRINITY

Now that the day has come to a close, I thank you, O
   Lord, and I entreat that the evening with the night
   may be restful;

Grant this to me, O Savior, and save me.

Now that the day has passed, I glorify you, O Master, and entreat that the evening with the night may be without offense;

Grant this to me, O Savior, and save me.

Now that the day has run its course, I praise you, O Holy One, and entreat that the evening with the night may be peaceful;

Grant this to me, O Savior, and save me.

CLOSING VERSES

Lord, your mercy endures forever; turn not away from the work of your hands.

To you is due praise, to you is due worship, to you is due glory, O Holy Trinity.

You who at all times and all hours in heaven and on earth are worshiped and glorified, O Christ our God, merciful and filled with compassion; who love the righteous and grant mercy to sinners; who call all people to salvation by the promise of future blessings: accept our prayer in this hour and guide our life toward your commandments.

Compline

In the Western tradition,
Compline is night prayer
prayed just before retiring.

May the all-powerful Lord
grant us a peaceful night. Amen.

> *(Pause for a short time to reflect on the activities of the day and see where you might have offended God in dealing wrongly with his creation.)*

I confess to almighty God,
and to you, my brothers and sisters,
that I have sinned through my own fault,
in my thoughts and in my words,
in what I have done,
and in what I have failed to do,
and I ask blessed Mary, ever virgin,
all the angels and saints,
and you, my brothers and sisters,
to pray for me to the Lord our God.

May almighty God have mercy on us,
forgive us our sins,
and bring us to everlasting life.
Amen.

O God, come to my assistance.
O Lord, make haste to help me.

Glory be to the Father
   and to the Son
   and to the Holy Spirit.
   As it was in the beginning,
   is now, and ever shall be,
   world without end. Amen.

PSALM 91

He who dwells in the shelter of the Most High
and abides in the shade of the Almighty
says to the Lord: 'My refuge,
my stronghold, my God in whom I trust.'

It is he who will free you from the snare
of the fowler who seeks to destroy you;
he will conceal you with his pinions
and under his wings you will find refuge.

You will not fear the terror of the night
nor the arrow that flies by day,
nor the plague that prowls in the darkness
nor the scourge that lays waste at noon.

Since he clings to me in love, I will free him;
protect him for he knows my name.
When he calls I shall answer: I am with you.
I will save him in distress and give him glory.

With length of life I will content him;
I shall let him see my saving power.

PSALM 134

O come, bless the Lord,
all you who serve the Lord,
who stand in the house of the Lord,
in the courts of the house of our God.

Lift up your hands to the holy place
and bless the Lord through the night.

May the Lord bless you from Zion,
he who made both heaven and earth.

(Pause for a few moments of reflection.)

AN EVENING HYMN

O Christ, you are the light and day
Which drives away the night,
The ever-shining Sun of God
And pledge of future light.

As now the evening shadows fall
Please grant us, Lord, we pray,
A quiet night to rest in you
Until the break of day.

Remember us, poor mortal ones,
We humbly ask, O Lord,
And may your presence in our souls
Be now our great reward.

VERSES OF PETITION

Into your hands, O Lord, I commend my spirit.
   You have redeemed me, O Lord, God of Truth.

Keep me, O Lord, as the pupil of your eye.
   Shelter me under the shadow of your wings.

CANTICLE OF SIMEON

Protect us, Lord, while we are awake and safeguard us while we sleep, that we may keep watch with Christ and rest in peace.

   Now Lord, you may dismiss your servant in peace,
      according to your word;
   For my eyes have seen your salvation
      which you have set before all the nations,
   As a light of revelation for the Gentiles
      and the glory of your people Israel.

Protect us, Lord, while we are awake and safeguard us while we sleep, that we may keep watch with Christ and rest in peace.

CLOSING PRAYER

Let us pray:

Visit this house, O Lord,
and guard us in peace.
Let your blessing rest upon us always.
This we ask in the name of Christ. Amen.

May the all-powerful and merciful Lord:
Father, Son and Holy Spirit,
bless and keep us.
Amen.

HYMN TO OUR LADY

Hail, Blessed Lady,
Mother most kind and merciful;
Fountain of goodness,
Hope of life immortal.

We are but sinners,
Children of Eve still in exile.
To you we send our sighs,
  the trials that befall us,
  passing through this vale of sorrow.

Hear then our plea as our intercessor,
Turn then to us those loving eyes compassionate,
  to give us comfort.

Then, Holy Maid, when our exile
  here on earth is ended,

still happier are those who hear the word of god and keep it.

LUKE 11:28

Lead us to Jesus Christ, your Son in glory.

O gentle,
O loving,
O gracious,
O Virgin Mary.

Pray for us, Holy Mother of God,
  that we may be made worthy
  of the promises of Christ.

Let us pray:

All powerful, eternal God, by the cooperation of the Holy Spirit you made ready the body and soul of the glorious Virgin Mother Mary to be a fit dwelling place for your Son. As we celebrate her memory with joy, grant that through her motherly intercession, we may be preserved from evil in this world and from eternal death. Through the same Christ, our Lord. Amen.

May the divine assistance
  remain always with us. Amen.

Vespers

Vatican Council II taught us that Vespers is one of the prayers upon which the day should hinge. The format presented here has recently been developed with the Council's teaching in mind.

O God, come to my assistance.
O Lord, make haste to help me.
Glory be to the Father
   and to the Son
   and to the Holy Spirit.
   As it was in the beginning,
   is now and ever shall be,
   world without end. Amen.

AN EVENING HYMN

O Light, O Trinity most blest.
True God, supreme and ever best:
As now the sun of day departs,
Outpour thy light upon our hearts.

To thee at morn our hymns we raise,
At evening offer prayer and praise;
And thou our glorious theme shall be,
Both now and through eternity.

As darkness deepens, Lord, do thou
A night of quiet rest bestow;
From all our sins grant us release,
And bless us with thy perfect peace.

PSALM 127:1-2

If the Lord does not build the house,
in vain do its builders labour;
if the Lord does not watch over the city,
in vain does the watchman keep vigil.

In vain is your earlier rising,
your going later to rest,

you who toil for the bread you eat:
when he pours gifts on his beloved while they slumber.

Give praise to the Father Almighty,
to his Son, Jesus Christ, the Lord,
to the Spirit who dwells in our hearts,
both now and for ages unending.

(Pause for reflection.)

PSALM 23

The Lord is my shepherd;
there is nothing I shall want.
Fresh and green are the pastures
where he gives me repose.
Near restful waters he leads me,
to revive my drooping spirit.

He guides me along the right path;
he is true to his name.
If I should walk in the valley of darkness,
no evil would I fear.
You are there with your crook and your staff;
with these you give me comfort.

You have prepared a banquet for me
in the sight of my foes.
My head you have anointed with oil;
my cup is overflowing.

Surely goodness and kindness shall follow me
all the days of my life.
In the Lord's own house shall I dwell
forever and ever.

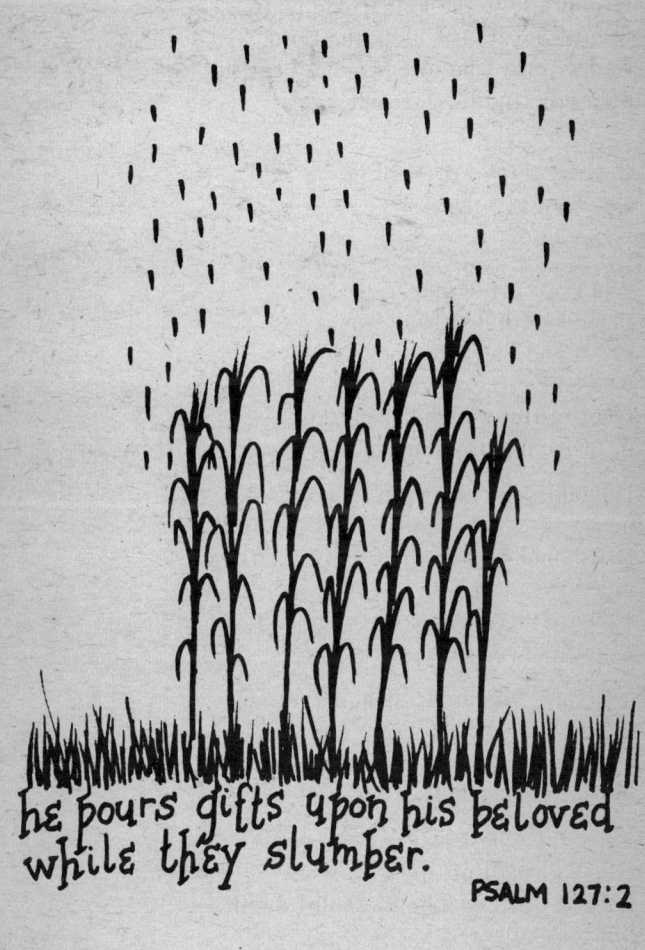

To the Father and Son give glory,
give glory to the Spirit.
To God who is, who was and who will be
forever and ever.

>   *(Pause for reflection.)*

PSALM 131

O Lord, my heart is not proud
nor haughty my eyes.
I have not gone after things too great
nor marvels beyond me.

Truly I have set my soul
in silence and peace.
A weaned child on its mother's breast,
even so is my soul.

O Israel, hope in the Lord
both now and forever.
Praise the Father, Son and Holy Spirit
forever. Amen.

>   *(Pause here to read briefly
>   from the holy scriptures. A
>   list of possible passages is
>   found at the end of this book.)*

OUR LADY'S HYMN

My soul glorifies the Lord,
  my spirit rejoices in God, my Savior.
He looks on his servant in her nothingness;
  henceforth all ages will call me blessed.
The Almighty works marvels for me.
  Holy his name.

His mercy is from age to age,
   on those who fear him.
He puts forth his arm in strength
   and scatters the proud-hearted.
He casts the mighty from their thrones,
   and raises the lowly.
He fills the starving with good things,
   sends the rich away empty.
He protects Israel his servant,
   remembering his mercy,
The mercy promised to our fathers,
   for Abraham and his sons forever.

Praise the Father, the Son and Holy Spirit,
   both now and forever, world without end.

> *(Pause again for a few moments of personal prayer, speaking to God from your heart in your own words. If several persons are praying together, they may wish to pray aloud, each in his/her own way.)*

CONCLUDING PRAYERS

Let us pray to God our Father
   as Jesus has taught us to pray:

Our Father . . . but deliver us from evil.

For thine is the Kingdom,
   and the power and the glory,
   now and forever. Amen.

Let us bless the Lord.
   Thanks be to God.

May the Lord bless us,
 may he keep us from all evil,
 and bring us to life everlasting.

Amen.

Thoughts for Evening Meditation

A selection of appropriate passages from many sources that speak to us of God's gift of evening and its restful refreshment.

O rest in the Lord; wait patiently for him,
and he shall give thee thy heart's desires.
Commit thy way unto him, and trust in him,
and fret not thyself because of evil doers.

F. Mendelssohn
Elijah

For thus said the Lord God,
   the Holy One of Israel:
In returning and rest shall you be saved,
   in quietness and in trust your strength lies.

Isaiah 30:15

If only I may grow: firmer, simpler—
   quieter, warmer.

Dag Hammarskjold
Markings

The words of the wise heard in quiet
   are better than the shouting
   of a ruler among fools.

Qoheleth 9:17

He will feed his flock like a shepherd,
   he will gather the lambs in his arms,
he will carry them in his bosom,
   and gently lead those that are with young.

Isaiah 40:11

Come to me, all you who are weary
and find life burdensome,
and I will refresh you.

No peace which is not peace for all,
no rest until all has been fulfilled.

> Dag Hammarskjold
> *Markings*

The just man enters into peace;
There is rest on his couch
   for the sincere, straightforward man.

> Isaiah 57:2

    When God at first made man,
Having a glasse of blessings standing by;
Let us (said he) poure on him all we can:
Let the worlds riches, which dispersed lie,
        Contract into a span.

    So strength first made a way;
Then beautie flow'd, then wisdome, honour, pleasure:
When almost all was out, God made a stay,
Perceiving that alone of all his treasure
        Rest in the bottome lay.

    For if I should (said he)
Bestow this jewell also on my creature,
He would adore my gifts instead of me,
And rest in Nature, not the God of Nature:
        So both should losers be.

    Yet let him keep the rest,
But keep them with repining restlessnesse:
Let him be rich and wearie, that at least,
If goodnesse leade him not, yet wearinesse
        May tosse him to my breast.

> George Herbert
> "The Pulley"

Take my yoke upon your shoulders
and learn from me,
for I am gentle and humble of heart.
Your souls will find rest,
for my yoke is easy
and my burden light.

Matthew 11:28-30

There is an appointed time for everything,
    and a time for every affair under the heavens.
A time to be born, and a time to die;
    a time to plant, and a time to uproot the plant.
A time to kill, and a time to heal;
    a time to tear down, and a time to build.
A time to weep, and a time to laugh;
    a time to mourn, and a time to dance.
A time to scatter stones, and a time to gather them;
    a time to embrace, and a time to be far from embraces.
A time to seek, and a time to lose;
    a time to keep, and a time to cast away.
A time to rend, and a time to sew;
    a time to be silent, and a time to speak.
A time to love, and a time to hate;
    a time of war and a time of peace.

Qoheleth 3:1-8

Time goes by: reputation increases,
    ability declines.

Dag Hammarskjold
Markings

I will make a covenant for them on that day
    with the beasts of the field,
    with the birds of the air,
    and with the things that crawl on the ground.

Bow and sword and war
   I will destroy from the land,
And I will let them take their rest in security.

I will espouse you to me forever;
I will espouse you in right and in justice;
   in love and in mercy;
I will espouse you in fidelity
   and you shall know the Lord.

Hosea 2:20-21

Thus says the Lord:
Stand beside the roads and look,
   ask the ancient paths which is the way to good,
   and walk it;
Thus will you find rest for your souls.

Jeremiah 6:16

Never "for the sake of peace and quiet,"
deny your own experience or convictions.

Dag Hammarskjold
Markings

To preserve the silence within—amid all the noise. To remain open and quiet, a moist humus in the fertile darkness where the rain falls and the grain ripens—no matter how many tramp across the parade ground in whirling dust under an arid sky.

Dag Hammarskjold
Markings

The apostles returned to Jesus and reported to him all that they had done and what they had taught. He said to them, "Come by yourselves to an out-of-the-way place and rest a little."

Mark 6:30-31

a moist humus... where the rain falls and the grain ripens.

HAMMARSKJOLD

I have no peace nor ease;
   I have no rest, for trouble comes!

But as for me, I know that my redeemer lives,
   and that he will at last stand forth upon the earth;
Whom I myself shall see:
   my own eyes, not another's, shall behold him,
And from my flesh I shall see God;
   my inmost being is consumed with longing.

Job 3:26; 19:25-27

Because there is in you the Glory, as our Lord's passion and resurrection have defined it, there will be in you a deep sensitivity, blended with a deep serenity. In your service of others, you will feel, you will care, you will be hurt, you will have your heart broken. And it is doubtful if any of us can do anything at all until we have been very much hurt, and until our hearts have been very much broken. And that is because God's gift to us is the glory of Christ crucified—being really sensitive to the pain and sorrow that does exist in so much of the world.

With this, a serenity that is deep in you—and because it is deep in you, it brings to others peace and healing. "Peace I leave with you. My peace I give to you." The life of a Christian ought to be like the ocean, with the surface constantly battered about by storms, but miles and miles below, deep peace, unmoved tranquillity.

Dr. Michael Ramsey
Archbishop of Canterbury
To the 1963 Congress of
the British Student
Christian Movement

By now they were near the village to which they were going, and he acted as if he were going farther. But they pressed him: "Stay with us. It is nearly evening—the day is practically over." So he went in to stay with them.

When he had seated himself with them to eat, he took bread, pronounced the blessing, then broke the bread and began to distribute it to them. With that their eyes were opened and they recognized him.

Luke 24:28-31

How gracious is the Lord;
our God has compassion.
The Lord protects the simple hearts;
I was helpless so he saved me.

Turn back, my soul, to your rest
for the Lord has been good.

Psalm 116:5-7

I am the vessel. The draught is God's.
And God is the thirsty one.

Dag Hammarskjold
Markings

You have been told, O man, what is good,
    and what the Lord requires of you:
Only to act justly, to love tenderly
    and to walk humbly with your God.

Micah 6:8

Though the fig trees do not blossom,
    nor fruit be on the vines,
the produce of the olive fail

and the fields yield no food,
the flock be cut off from the fold
and there be no herd in the stalls,
yet I will rejoice in the Lord,
I will joy in the God of my salvation.
God, the Lord, is my strength.

Habakkuk 3:17-19

O my God, I call by day and you give no reply;
I call by night and I find no peace.
Yet you, O God, are holy,
enthroned on the praises of Israel.

In you our fathers put their trust;
they trusted and you set them free.
When they cried to you, they escaped.
In you they trusted and never in vain.

Psalm 22

Then I saw a new heaven and a new earth. The former heaven and the former earth had passed away, and the sea was no more. I also saw a new Jerusalem, the holy city, coming down out of heaven from God, beautiful as a bride prepared to meet her husband. I heard a loud voice from the throne cry out: "This is God's dwelling among men. He shall dwell with them and they shall be his people and he shall be their God who is always with them. He shall wipe every tear from their eyes, and there shall be no more death or mourning, crying out or pain, for the former things have passed away."

Revelation 21:1-4

If we only have love, then Jerusalem stands!

Jacques Brel

Lead me, Lord, lead me in thy righteousness,
Make thy way plain before my face.
For it is thou, Lord, thou Lord only,
That makest me dwell in safety.

After Psalm 5:8; 4:9

Have peace in your heart
and thousands around you will be saved.

Seraphim of Sarov

if we only have love then Jerusalem stands.

J. BREL

The Lord has broken the rod of the wicked,
  the staff of the tyrants
That struck the peoples in wrath
  with relentless blows. . . .
The whole earth is at rest and quiet,
  they break forth into singing.

> Isaiah 14:5-7

And Moses said to the Lord, "Now, therefore, I pray you, if I have found favor in your sight, show me now your ways, that I may know you and find favor in your sight. Consider, too, that this nation is your people." The Lord answered: "My presence will go with you and I will give you rest."

> Exodus 33:14

Only he deserves power
who every day justifies it.

> Dag Hammarskjold
> *Markings*

May he who makes peace in all his vastness,
grant peace unto us,
and all Israel,
and all mankind,
and let us say: Amen. Amen.

> From the Passover Haggadah

Litanies of Praise

Praying to God and the saints in litany form has been a long tradition in many religious heritages. Those found here are collected from different sources:

The Litanies to Jesus are taken from the *Eikoi* of the "*Akathist* to our Lord Jesus Christ" prayed in the Eastern tradition.

The Litany known as the *Benedicite* comes from the Old Testament (Daniel 3). It is the song sung by Shadrack, Meshach and Abednego in the flames of the furnace of the king of Babylon.

The Litany of Loretto (to the Mother of God) was approved for the Western Church by Pope Sixtus V in 1587.

The Litany of Peace is adapted from the Orthodox Divine Liturgy of St. John Chrysostom.

The *Preces*, or Prayers, were part of the Lenten Office of the Roman Breviary.

Jesus, Eternal God!
Jesus, King of Kings!
Jesus, Lord of Lords!
Jesus, Judge of the living and the dead!
Jesus, Hope of the hopeless!
Jesus, Comforter of the mournful!
Jesus, Glory of the poor!
Jesus, condemn me not according to my deeds!
Jesus, cleanse me according to your mercy!
Jesus, take from me despondency!
Jesus, enlighten the thoughts of my heart!
Jesus, make me ever mindful of death!
Jesus, Son of God, have mercy on me!

> Blessed are you, O Lord, the God of our fathers,
>   praiseworthy and exalted above all forever:
> And blessed is your holy and glorious name,
>   praiseworthy and exalted above all forever;
> Blessed are you in the temple of your glory,
>   praiseworthy and exalted above all forever;
> Blessed are you on the throne of your kingdom,
>   praiseworthy and exalted above all forever;
> Blessed are you in the firmament of heaven,
>   praiseworthy and exalted above all forever.

Jesus, Uncontainable Word!
Jesus, Inscrutable Intelligence!
Jesus, Incomprehensible Power!
Jesus, Inconceivable Wisdom!

Jesus, Undepictable Deity!
Jesus, Boundless Dominion!
Jesus, Invincible Kingdom!
Jesus, Unending Sovereignty!
Jesus, Supreme Strength!
Jesus, Eternal Power!
Jesus, my Creator, have compassion on me!
Jesus, my Savior, save me!
Jesus, Son of God, have mercy on me!

    Bless the Lord, all you works of the Lord,
        praise and exalt him above all forever.
    Angels of the Lord, bless the Lord,
    You heavens, bless the Lord,
    All you waters above the heavens, bless the Lord,
    All you hosts of the Lord, bless the Lord,
        praise and exalt him above all forever.

    Sun and moon, bless the Lord,
    Stars of heaven, bless the Lord,
    Every shower and dew, bless the Lord,
    All you winds, bless the Lord,
        praise and exalt him above all forever.

    Fire and heat, bless the Lord,
    Cold and chill, bless the Lord,
    Dew and rain, bless the Lord,
    Frost and chill, bless the Lord,
    Ice and snow, bless the Lord,
        praise and exalt him above all forever.

    Nights and days, bless the Lord,
    Light and darkness, bless the Lord,
    Lightnings and clouds, bless the Lord,
    Let all the earth bless the Lord,
        praise and exalt him above all forever.

Mountains and hills, bless the Lord,
Everything growing from the earth, bless the Lord.
You springs, bless the Lord,
Seas and rivers, bless the Lord,
You dolphins and all water creatures, bless the Lord.
All you birds of the air, bless the Lord,
All you beasts, wild and tame, bless the Lord,
  praise and exalt him above all forever.

You sons of men, bless the Lord,
O Israel, bless the Lord,
Priests of the Lord, bless the Lord,
Servants of the Lord, bless the Lord,
Spirits and souls of the just, bless the Lord,
Holy men of humble heart, bless the Lord,
  praise and exalt him above all forever.

Jesus, True God!
Jesus, Son of David!
Jesus, Glorious King!
Jesus, Innocent Lamb!
Jesus, Wonderful Shepherd!
Jesus, Guardian of my infancy!
Jesus, Nourisher of my youth!
Jesus, Praise of my old age!
Jesus, my hope at death!
Jesus, my Life after death!
Jesus, my Comfort at your Judgment!
Jesus, my Desire, let me not then be ashamed!
Jesus, Son of God, have mercy on me!

THE LITANY OF LORETTO

Lord, have mercy.
Christ, have mercy.

Lord, have mercy.
Christ, hear us.
Christ, graciously hear us.
God the Father of heaven, have mercy on us.
God the Son, Redeemer of the world, have mercy on us.
God the Holy Spirit, have mercy on us.
Holy Trinity, one God, have mercy on us.
Holy Mary, pray for us.
Holy Mother of God, pray for us, etc.
Holy Virgin of virgins,
Mother of Christ,
Mother of divine grace,
Mother most pure,
Mother most chaste,
Mother inviolate,
Mother undefiled,
Mother most amiable,
Mother most admirable,
Mother of good counsel,
Mother of our Creator,
Mother of our Savior,
Virgin most prudent,
Virgin most venerable,
Virgin most renowned,
Virgin most powerful,
Virgin most merciful,
Virgin most faithful,
Mirror of justice,
Seat of wisdom,
Cause of our joy,
Spiritual vessel,
Vessel of honor,
Singular vessel of devotion,

Mystical rose,
Tower of David,
Tower of ivory,
House of gold,
Ark of the covenant,
Gate of heaven,
Morning star,
Health of the sick,
Refuge of sinners,
Comfort of the afflicted,
Help of Christians,
Queen of angels,
Queen of patriarchs,
Queen of prophets,
Queen of apostles,
Queen of martyrs,
Queen of confessors,
Queen of virgins,
Queen of all saints,
Queen conceived without original sin,
Queen assumed into heaven,
Queen of the most holy rosary,
Queen of peace.

Lamb of God, who takes away the sins of the world,
    spare us, O Lord.
Lamb of God, who takes away the sins of the world,
    graciously hear us, O Lord.
Lamb of God, who takes away the sins of the world,
    have mercy on us.

Pray for us, Holy Mother of God.
    That we may be made worthy
    of the promises of Christ.

Let us pray:

Grant us your servants, we beseech you, O Lord God, to enjoy perpetual health of mind and body, that through the glorious intercession of the blessed Mary ever Virgin, we may be delivered from present sorrow, and enjoy everlasting happiness. Through Christ our Lord. Amen.

> Jesus, Creator of those on high!
> Jesus, Redeemer of those below!
> Jesus, Vanquisher of the powers of evil!
> Jesus, Adorner of every creature!
> Jesus, Comforter of my soul!
> Jesus, Enlightener of my mind!
> Jesus, Gladness of my heart!
> Jesus, Health of my body!
> Jesus, my Savior, save me!
> Jesus, my Light, enlighten me!
> Jesus, deliver me from all suffering!
> Jesus, save me despite my unworthiness!
> Jesus, Son of God, have mercy on me!

THE LITANY OF PEACE

Again and again in peace,
let us pray to the Lord.

> Lord, have mercy.

For the peace from above
and for the salvation of our souls,
let us pray to the Lord.

> Lord, have mercy.

For peace in the whole world,
the welfare of the holy churches of God,
and the union of all men,
let us pray to the Lord.

> Lord, have mercy.

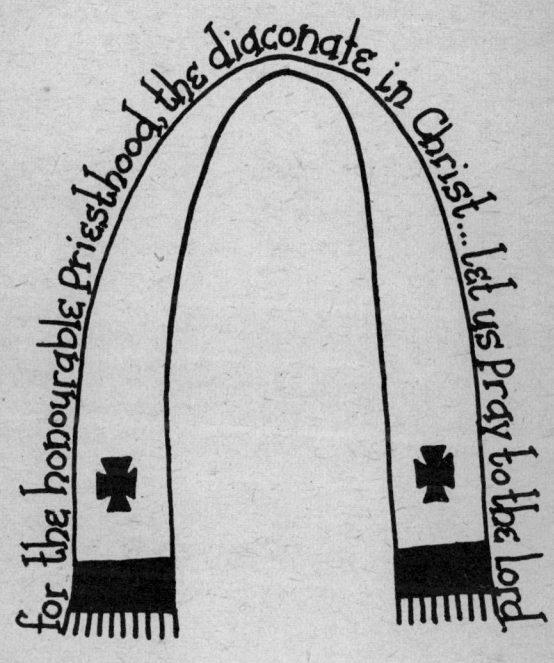

LITANY OF PEACE

For this holy church
and for those who enter it with faith,
reverence and the fear of God,
let us pray to the Lord.

                                      Lord, have mercy.

For our Holy Father and all the patriarchs,
our bishop (name),
for the honorable priesthood,
the diaconate in Christ,
and for all the clergy and the people,
let us pray to the Lord.

                                      Lord, have mercy.

For our country, our President, our Congress,
and all in seats of authority,
let us pray to the Lord.

                                      Lord, have mercy.

For this city and for every city and land,
and for those who live in them by faith,
let us pray to the Lord.

                                      Lord, have mercy.

For seasonable weather,
the abundance of the fruits of the earth,
and peaceful times,
let us pray to the Lord.

                                      Lord, have mercy.

For those who travel by land, air, and water,
for the sick, the suffering,
for prisoners and captives,
and for their salvation,
let us pray to the Lord.

                                      Lord, have mercy.

That he will deliver us from all tribulation,
anger, danger and want,
let us pray to the Lord.

                                        Lord, have mercy.

Help us, save us, have mercy on us,
and keep us, O God, by your grace.

                                        Lord, have mercy.

Remembering our most holy, most pure,
most blessed and glorious Lady,
Mother of God and ever-Virgin Mary,
with all the saints,
let us entrust ourselves and one another
and all our life to Christ, our God.

                                        To you, O Lord.

For to you belongs
all glory, honor and adoration,
to the Father, and to the Son,
and to the Holy Spirit, now and ever,
and to the ages of ages.

                                        Amen.

THE PRECES

I said: O Lord, be merciful to me.
    Heal my soul, for I have sinned against you.

Will you turn again to us, O Lord, at last?
    And be ready to hear the entreaties of your servants?

Let your mercy, Lord, spread over us.
    As we have hoped in you.

Let your priests be clothed with justice,
    And let your saints rejoice.

Let us pray for our Holy Father Pope (name).
   May the Lord preserve him and give him life
   and make him blessed on earth,
   and not deliver him up to the will of his enemies.

Let us pray for our bishop (name).
   May he stand firm and shepherd his flock
   by your strength, O Lord,
   in the majesty of your name.

O Lord, save the President.
   And listen to us when we call upon you.

Save your people, Lord, and bless your inheritance.
   And rule them, and exalt them forever.

Remember your congregation.
   Which you have possessed from the beginning.

Let there be peace in your strength.
   And abundance in your towers.

Let us pray for our benefactors.
   May you see fit, Lord,
   to bestow eternal life on all those
   who do good to us for your sake. Amen.

Let us pray for the faithful departed.
   Eternal rest grant to them, O Lord,
   and let perpetual light shine upon them.

May they rest in peace.
   Amen.

For those who are absent from us.
   Save your servants who hope in you, my God.

For those in affliction and in captivity.
   Deliver them, O God of Israel,
   out of all their troubles.

Send them help, O Lord, from the sanctuary.
  And out of Sion defend them.

O Lord, God of Hosts, give us a change of heart.
  Face us lovingly, and we shall be saved.

Arise, O Christ, and help us.
  And deliver us for your name's sake.

O Lord, hear my prayer.
  And let my cry come to you.

Evening Prayer for the Sabbath

These prayers are adapted from the ancient Jewish custom of kindling the Sabbath lights. Jews do this on Friday evening, the beginning of their Sabbath. Christians could imitate this beautiful custom by doing it at the evening meal on Saturday. But it could also be done at Sunday dinner. The table is prepared with candles and the meal should be festive and relaxed.

The ceremony begins with the woman of the house lighting the candles and saying:

> Blessed are you, O Lord our God,
> King of the universe,
> who makes us holy with your Presence
> and enlightens the world with your Glory.

The man of the house then reads the following passage from the Book of Genesis:

Evening came, and morning followed—the sixth day. Thus the heavens and the earth and all their array were completed. Since on the seventh day God was finished with the work he had been doing, he rested on the seventh day from all the work he had undertaken.

He then continues:

> Blessed are you, O Lord our God, King of the universe, who has made us holy by your commandments and has taken pleasure in us, and in love and favor has given us your holy Sabbath as an inheritance, a memorial of creation. For you have chosen us and sanctified us above all nations, and in love and favor have given us your holy Sabbath as an inheritance. Blessed are you, O Lord, who makes holy the Sabbath.

All respond:

> Amen. Amen.

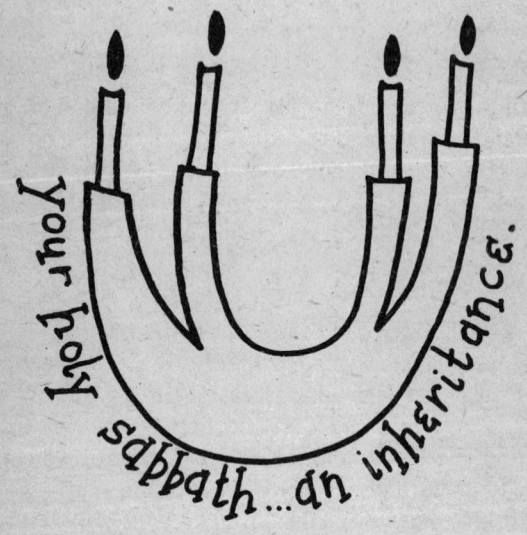

Other readings for the Sabbath:

Take care to keep holy the Sabbath day as the Lord, your God, commanded you. Six days you may labor and do all your work; but the seventh day is the Sabbath of the Lord, your God. No work may be done then, whether by you, or your son or daughter, or your male or female slave, or your ox or ass or any of your beasts, or the alien who lives with you . . . For remember that you too were once slaves in Egypt, and the Lord, your God, brought you from there with his strong hand and outstretched arm. That is why the Lord, your God, has commanded you to observe the Sabbath day.

Deuteronomy 5:12-15

Come, my friend, to meet the bride;
let us welcome the Sabbath.

> Come, let us go to meet the Sabbath,
> for it is a source of blessing.
> From the beginning it was ordained;
> last in creation, first in God's plan.

Come, my friend, to meet the bride;
let us welcome the Sabbath.

> Come in peace, crown of God,
> come with joy and cheerfulness.

Come, my friend, to meet the bride;
let us welcome the Sabbath.

Rabbi Alkabetz, 1540
Lechoh dodi

Prayers for Special Evenings

Two evenings of the year are most sacred
in the Christian life: Christmas Eve and
the Vigil of Easter. These prayers are
from the Church's liturgy for these evenings.

CHRISTMAS EVE

Father, you make this holy night radiant with the splendor of Jesus Christ our light. We welcome him as Lord, the true light of the world. Bring us to eternal joy in the kingdom of heaven, where he lives and reigns with you in the Holy Spirit, one God forever and ever.

Prayer for Midnight Mass

When he came to us as man, the Son of God scattered the darkness of this world, and filled this holy night with his glory. May the God of infinite goodness scatter the darkness of sin and brighten your hearts with holiness. Amen.

A Christmas Blessing

Lord our God, with the birth of your Son, your glory breaks on the world. Through the night hours of the darkened earth, we your people watch for the coming of your promised Son. As we wait, give us a foretaste of the joy that you will grant us when the fullness of his glory has filled the earth, who lives and reigns with you forever and ever. Amen.

Another Prayer for Midnight Mass

Almighty God and Father of light, a child is born for us and a son is given to us. Your eternal Word leaped down from heaven in the silent watches of the night, and now your church is filled with wonder at the nearness of her God. Open our hearts to receive his life and increase our vision with the rising of dawn, that our

lives may be filled with his glory and his peace, who lives and reigns forever and ever. Amen.

Prayer for the Mass at Dawn

THE VIGIL OF EASTER

Lord God, you have brightened this night with the radiance of the risen Christ. Quicken the spirit of sonship in your church; renew us in mind and body to give you wholehearted service.

Easter Collect

(The Easter candle in the home is lighted and the following great hymn is proclaimed:)

It is truly right
that with full hearts and minds and voices
we should praise the unseen God,
the all-powerful Father,
and his only Son, our Lord Jesus Christ.

For Christ has ransomed us with his blood
   and paid for us the price of Adam's sin
   to our eternal Father!

This is the passover feast,
   when Christ, the true Lamb, is slain,
   whose blood consecrates the homes
   of all believers.

This is the night when first you saved our fathers:
   you freed the people of Israel from their slavery
   and led them dry-shod through the sea.

This is the night when the pillar of fire
   destroyed the darkness of sin!

This is the night when Christians everywhere,
  washed clean of sin
  and freed from all defilement,
  are restored to grace and grow together
  in holiness.

This is the night when Jesus Christ
  broke the chains of death
  and rose triumphant from the grave.

What good would life have been to us,
  had Christ not come as our Redeemer?

Father, how wonderful your care for us!
  How boundless your merciful love!
  To ransom a slave
  you gave away your Son.

O happy fault, O necessary sin of Adam,
  which gained for us so great a redeemer!

Most blest of all nights, chosen by God
  to see Christ rising from the dead!

Of this night Scripture says:
  "This night will be as clear as day:
  it will become my light, my joy."

The power of this holy night
  dispels all evil, washes guilt away,
  restores lost innocence, brings mourners joy;
  it casts out hatred, brings us peace,
  and humbles earthly pride.

Night truly blest when heaven is wedded to earth
    and man is reconciled with God!

Therefore, heavenly Father,
    in the joy of this night,
    receive our evening sacrifice of praise,
    your church's solemn offering.

Accept this Easter candle,
    a flame divided but undimmed,
    a pillar of fire that glows to the honor of God.

Let it mingle with the lights of heaven
    and continue bravely burning
    to dispel the darkness of this night!

May the morning star which never sets
    find this flame still burning:
    Christ, that morning star,
    who came back from the dead,
    and shed his peaceful light on all mankind,
    your Son who lives and reigns
    forever and ever. Amen.

From the "Exultet"

this is the night when christ rose triumphant

Other Prayers for Evening

A sampling of short evening prayers written by Christians down through the ages.

Lord, may I be wakeful at sunrise to begin a new day for you; cheerful at sunset for having done my work for you; thankful at moonrise and under starshine for the beauty of your universe. And may I add what little may be in me to add to your great world.

The Abbot of Greve

Bless all who worship you, O Lord, from the rising of the sun even to its going down. Of your goodness, give us; with your love, inspire us; by your Spirit, guide us; by your power, protect us; in your mercy receive us now and always.

An Ancient Collect

Now at the daylight's ending
We turn, O God to you:
Send forth your Holy Spirit,
Our spirit now renew.

To you in adoration,
In thankfulness and praise,
In faith and hope and gladness,
Our loving hearts we raise.

The gift you gave at daylight
This night you take away,
To leave within our keeping
The blessings of this day.

Take all its joy and sorrow,
Take all that love can give,
But all that needs forgiveness,
Dear Father, now forgive.

With watchful eyes, O Shepherd,
Look down upon your sheep;
Stretch forth your hand in healing
And close our eyes in sleep.

Come down, O Holy Spirit,
To be our loving Guest;
Be near us, holy angels,
And guard us as we rest.

We praise you, heav'nly Father:
From you all light descends;
You give us heaven's glory
When life's brief daylight ends.

We praise you, Jesus, Savior,
The light of heav'n above;
We praise you, Holy Spirit,
The living flame of love.

James Quinn, S.J.

Almighty God, we give you thanks for bringing us safely to this evening hour. May this lifting up of our hands in prayer be a sacrifice pleasing in your sight.

Evening Prayer
Liturgy of the Hours, 1975

Lord, may our evening prayer rise up to you,
and your blessing come down upon us.

Evening Prayer
Liturgy of the Hours, 1975

Lord Jesus Christ, abide with us,
Now that the sun has run its course;

Let hope not be obscured by night,
But may faith's darkness be as light.

Lord Jesus Christ, grant us your peace,
And when the trials of earth shall cease,
Grant us the morning light of grace,
The radiant splendor of your face.

Immortal, Holy, Threefold Light,
Yours be the Kingdom, pow'r, and might.
All glory be eternally
To you, life-giving Trinity!

Jerome Leaman

Almighty Father, you have given us the strength to work throughout this day. Receive our evening sacrifice of praise in thanksgiving for your countless gifts.

Evening Prayer
Liturgy of the Hours, 1975

Lord, fill this night with your radiance.
May we sleep in peace and rise with joy
to welcome the light of a new day in your name.

Evening Prayer
Liturgy of the Hours, 1975

Inspiring light, O holy glory
of the undying, heavenly Father,
the holy, the blessed Jesus Christ:
the sun has set and now, seeing the lamp
that lights the evening,
we praise the Father and the Son
and God the Holy Spirit.

Praise is yours at all times
from dutiful lips,
O Son of God, O Giver of life;
therefore does the world give you glory.

*The "Phos Hilaron" of
the Greek Church*

Abide with me,
Fast falls the eventide;
The darkness deepens;
Lord, abide with me:
When other helpers fail,
And comforts flee,
Help of the helpless,
O abide with me.

H. F. Lyte, 1847

Be present, O merciful God, and protect us through the silent hours of this night, so that we who are wearied by the changes and chances of this fleeting world may repose upon your eternal changelessness, through Jesus Christ, our Lord.

Leonine Sacramentary

O God, with whom there is no darkness, but the night shines as the day: keep and defend us and all your children, we beseech you, throughout the coming night. Renew our hearts with your forgiveness and our bodies with untroubled sleep, that we may wake to use more faithfully your gift of life, through Jesus Christ, our Lord.

Parish Prayers

Watch, dear Lord, with those who wake, or watch, or weep tonight, and take charge over those who sleep. Tend your sick ones, O Lord Christ; rest your weary ones; bless your dying ones; soothe your suffering ones; pity your afflicted ones; shield your joyous ones. And all for your name's sake. Amen.

Augustine

Lord God, heavenly Father,
Use the quiet of this night
   to settle the hearts of men everywhere,
   that they may contemplate
   your goodness and your mercy.
Still the strife that enters homes,
   communities, and nations.
Put down those who employ
   power for power's sake.
Stifle the mouths of those
   who foment bigotry and hate.
Pour out your love in fullness
   upon those who honor your name,
   that your kingdom may come
   and your will may be done among us,
   for Jesus' sake. Amen.

Lutheran Book of Prayer

We, your thankful and unworthy servants, praise and glorify you, O Lord, for your great benefits which we have received this day; we bless you, we thank you, we sing to you and we magnify your great goodness, and in lowliness and love we hymn you: O Benefactor and Savior, glory to you.

Prayer of the Greek Church

O Lord, support us all the day long of this troubled life until the shadows lengthen and the evening comes, and the busy world is hushed, and the fever of life is over, and our work is done. Then in your mercy grant us a safe lodging and a holy rest, and peace at the last. Amen.

John Henry Newman

Holy Father,
We glorify your name
   because you give rest to the weary.
Strengthen this night
   all who are worn from the burdens of labor.
Relieve through him who died for all
   those who are sick and dying.
Comfort with the news of the resurrection
   those who mourn.
Counsel with the wisdom of your love
   those who are in difficulty.
Cheer with the joy of salvation
   those who are depressed.
Renew with the assurance of your presence
   those who are lonely.
Send the angels of your mercy
   to those who are distressed.
Reach out to all men this night
   with the healing and redeeming love
   of Christ, our Lord. Amen.

Lutheran Book of Prayer

All praise to you, my God, this night
For all the blessings of the light;
Keep me, O keep me, King of Kings,
Beneath thine own almighty wings.

Upon the twilight chaos played,
Your wisdom forming night and day.
As night descends to you we sing
To hover near on brooding wing.

Forgive me, Lord, for your dear Son,
The ill that I this day have done;
That with the world, myself and thee,
Before I sleep, at peace may be.

Almighty Father, hear our cry,
Through Jesus Christ our Lord most high,
Whom in the Spirit we adore
Who reigns with you forevermore.

Thomas Ken, 1680

O Lord, grant me to greet the coming day in peace. Help me in all things to rely upon your holy will. In every hour of the day reveal your will to me. Bless my dealings with all who surround me. Teach me to treat all that come to me throughout the day with peace of soul and with the firm conviction that your will governs all. In all my deeds and words guide my thoughts and feelings. In unforeseen events let me not forget that all are sent by you. Teach me to act firmly and wisely, without embittering and embarrassing others. Give me the strength to bear the fatigue of the coming day with all that it shall bring. Direct my will, teach me to pray, and pray yourself in me. Amen.

Philaret of Moscow

Lord, make me an instrument of thy peace;
Where there is hatred, let me sow love;
Where there is injury, pardon;

Where there is discord, union;
Where there is doubt, faith;
Where there is despair, hope;
Where there is darkness, light;
Where there is sadness, joy.

O Divine Master, grant that I may not so much
Seek to be consoled, as to console;
To be understood, as to understand;
To be loved, as to love;
For it is in giving that we receive,
It is in pardoning that we are pardoned,
And it is in dying that we are born
To eternal life.

Francis of Assisi

We praise and thank you, O God, for you are without beginning and without end;
Through Christ you are the Creator and Preserver of the whole world, but above all, you are our God and Father, the Giver of the Spirit, and the Ruler of all that is seen and unseen.
You made the day for the works of light and the night for the refreshment of our weakness.
O loving Lord and Source of all that is good, mercifully accept our evening sacrifice of praise.
As you have helped us through the day and brought us to night's beginning, keep us now in Christ, grant us a peaceful evening, and a night free from sin, and at the end bring us to everlasting life,
Through Christ our Lord.

Apostolic Constitutions, 380

The day you gave us, Lord, has ended,
The darkness falls at your behest,
To you our morning hymns ascended,
Your praise shall sanctify our rest.

We thank you for the church unsleeping,
While earth rolls onward into light,
Through all the world her watch is keeping,
And never rests by day or night.

As over continent and island
The dawn leads in another day,
The voice of prayer is never silent,
Nor dies the sound of praise away.

Your endless might and power shall never,
Like earthly empires, fade away,
Your kingdom lives and grows forever
And all the worlds your power obey.

After St. Clement

Now on land and sea descending,
Brings the night its peace profound;
Let our vesper hymn be blending
With the holy calm around.
    Jubilate! Jubilate! Jubilate! Amen!
Let our vesper hymn be blending
With the holy calm around.

Soon as dies the sunset glory,
Stars of heaven shine out above,
Telling still the ancient story—
Their Creator's changeless love.
    Jubilate! Jubilate! Jubilate! Amen!

Telling still the ancient story—
Their Creator's changeless love.

Now our wants and burdens leaving
To his care who cares for all,
Cease we fearing, cease we grieving:
At his touch our burdens fall.
    Jubilate! Jubilate! Jubilate! Amen!
Cease we fearing, cease we grieving:
At his touch our burdens fall.

As the darkness deepens o'er us,
Lo! eternal stars arise;
Hope and faith and love rise glorious,
Shining in the Master's skies.
    Jubilate! Jubilate! Jubilate! Amen!
Hope and faith and love rise glorious,
Shining in the Master's skies.

Vesper Hymn (Bortniansky)
S. Longfellow, 1859, alt.

Now the day is over,
Night is drawing nigh,
Shadows of the evening
Steal across the sky.

Jesus, give the weary
Calm and sweet repose;
With your tender blessings
May my eyelids close.

S. Baring-Gould, 1865

We praise and thank you, O God, through your Son Jesus Christ our Lord, through whom you have enlightened us, by revealing the light that never fades.

Night is falling, and day's allotted span draws to a close.
The daylight which you created for our pleasure has fully satisfied us; and yet, of your free gift, now the evening lights do not fail us.
We praise you and glorify you through your Son, Jesus Christ, our Lord.

St. Hippolytus
Apostolic Tradition, c. 215

The setting sun now dies away,
And darkness comes at close of day;
Your brightest beams, dear Lord, impart,
And let them shine within our heart.

We praise your name with joy this night:
Please watch and guide us till the light;
Joining the music of the blest,
O Lord, we sing ourselves to rest.

Jam sol recedit igneus, 1706
trans. G. Laycock

Day is done,
But Love unfailing,
Dwells ever here;
Shadows fall,
But hope prevailing,
Calms every fear.
Loving Father,
None forsaking,
Take our hearts
Of Love's own making.
Watch our sleeping,
Guard our waking,
Be always near.

Dark descends,
But Light unending
Shines through the night;
You are with us,
Ever leading
New strength to sight;
One in love,
Your truth confessing,
One in hope
Of heaven's blessing.
May we see,
In love's possessing,
Love's endless light!

James Quinn, S.J.

O Lord, I know not what to ask of you this night. You alone know what are my true needs. You love me more than I myself know how to love. Help me see my real needs which are concealed from me. I dare not ask either a cross or consolation. I can only wait for you. My heart is open to you. Visit and help me, for your great name's sake. Strike me and heal me, cast me down and raise me up. I worship in silence your holy will and your inscrutable ways. I offer myself as a sacrifice to you. I put all my trust in you. I have no other desire than to fulfill your will. Teach me how to pray. Pray yourself in me. Amen.

Philaret of Moscow

Personal Favorite Prayers

The following pages are provided to permit you to write in or paste in your own personal favorite prayers.

Personal Favorite Prayers

Personal Favorite Prayers

Personal Favorite Prayers

Personal Favorite Prayers

Personal Favorite Prayers

Personal Favorite Prayers

Personal Favorite Prayers

Personal Favorite Prayers

Passages from Scripture

Genesis 1:1—2:4
        17:1-22
        22:1-19
        37:1-36
Exodus 14
      24
      32
Deuteronomy 30:15-20
Joshua 2
      6
      24
Judges 5
Ruth
1 Samuel 3
       17:32-51
2 Samuel 7
1 Kings 18
2 Kings 4:8-37
Nehemiah 9
Job 42:1-6
Proverbs 31
Ecclesiastes 3
Isaiah 5:1-7
     6:1-13
     7:1-17
     11:1-9
     40:1-5
     52:13—53:12
     55:10-11
     60:1-3
     61:1-4
Jeremiah 1:1-10
       31:31-34
Amos 8:4-10

Ezekiel 34:1-31
      37:1-14
Hosea 2:16-20
     11:1-12
Micah 6:8
Habakkuk 3:17-19
Zephaniah 3:14-20

Matthew 5:1-12
       6:26-34
       13:4-23
       14:13-21
       17:1-8
Luke 10:38-42
     16:1-13
     16:19-31
     19:1-10
John 1:1-18
     2:1-12
     6:1-15
     10:1-42
     14:1—17:26
     20:1-31
Acts 2:1-4
    2:42-47
Romans 4:1-8
       8:18-39
       14
1 Corinthians 13
Galatians 3:1-18
Ephesians 3:14-19
Hebrews 8:1-6
James 2:14-26
1 John 4:7-12